Giuseppe VERDI
LE TROUVÈRE
BALLET MUSIC
Edited by
Clark McAlister

Study Score
Partitur

SERENISSIMA MUSIC, INC.

ORCHESTRA

Flute

Piccolo

2 Oboes

2 Clarinets (A)

2 Bassoons

4 Horns (F)

2 Trumpets (B-flat)

2 Cornets (B-flat)

3 Trombones

Bass Trombone

Timpani

3 Percussion

Violins I

Violins II

Violas

Violoncellos

Double Basses

Duration: ca. 24 minutes
Premiere: January 12, 1857 (in Act III of the opera)
Paris, Salle Le Peleiier
Théâtre Impérial de l'Opéra
Théâtre Impérial Orchestra, Narcisse Girard (conductor)

© Copyright 2011 Clark McAlister
All rights reserved.

This study score is an unabridged reprint – in reduced format – of the large conductor's score first issued by Kalmus as number A9092. The large score (26123) and complete orchestra parts (26130) also available from Serenissima Music.

ISMN: 979-0-58042-102-9

LE TROUVÈRE
(IL TROVATORE)
Ballet Music

1. Pas de Bohèmiens

GIUSEPPE VERDI
Performing Edition by Clark McAlister

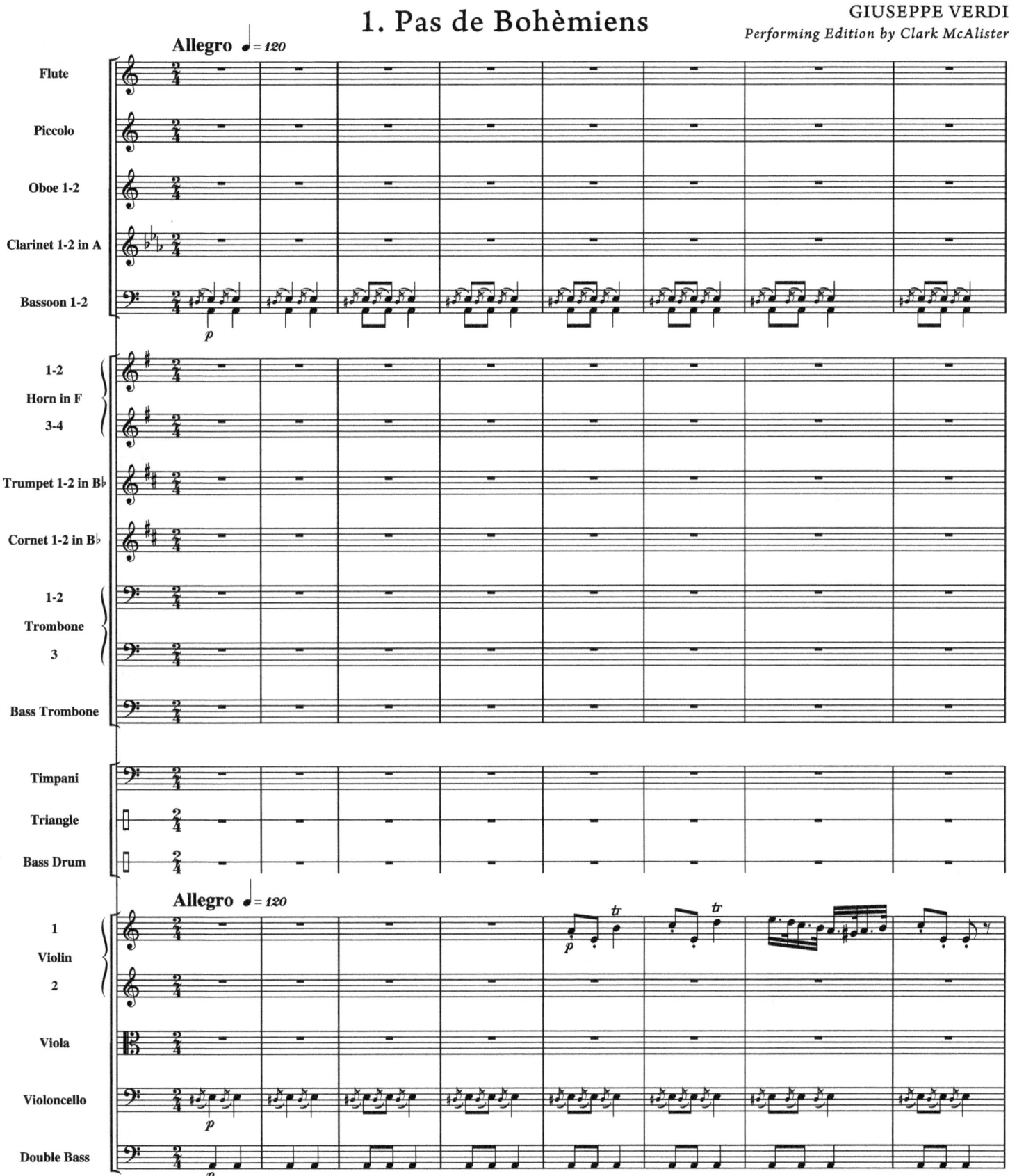

©Copyright 2011 Clark McAlister.

10

14

Gitanilla

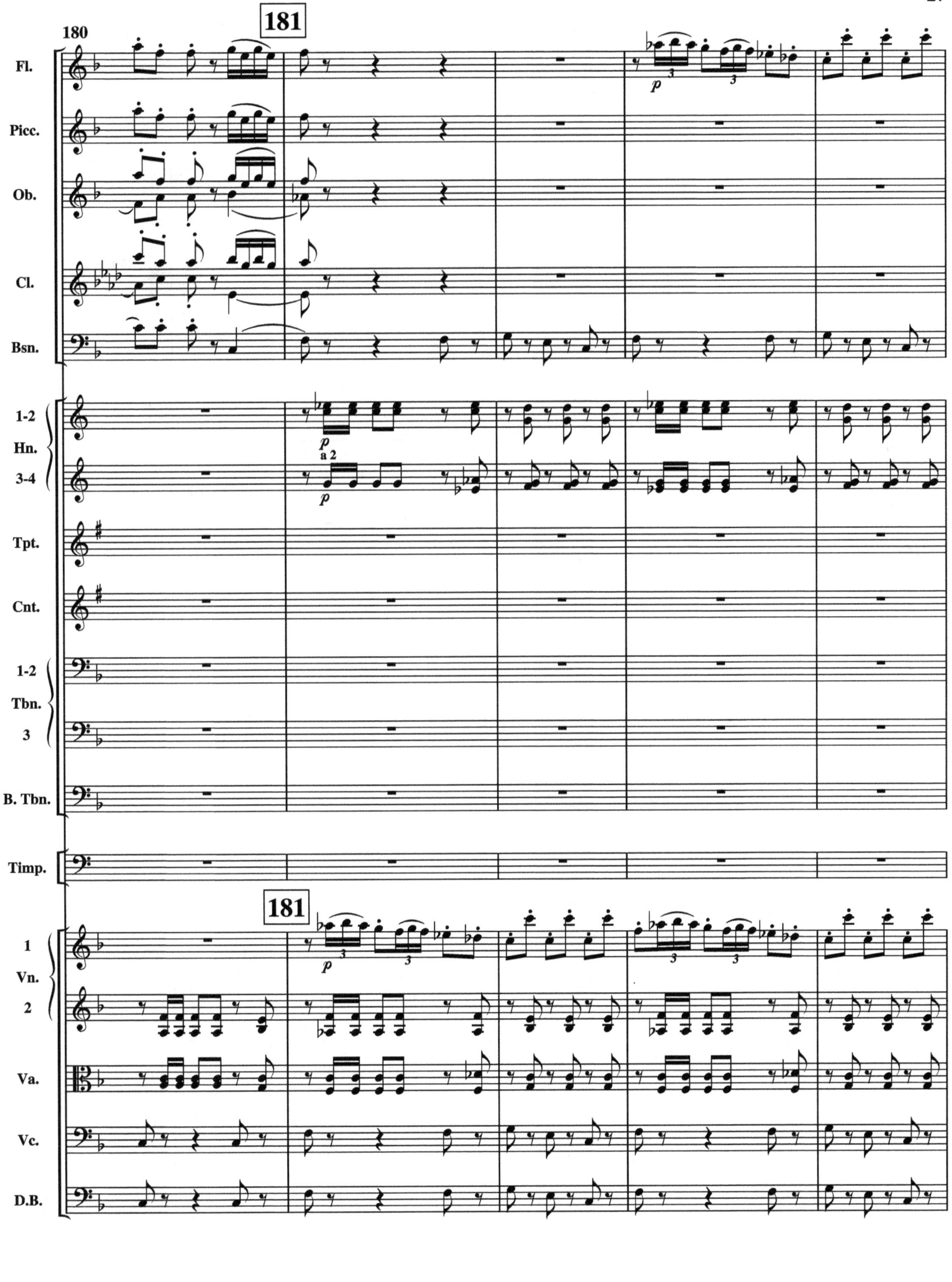
180
181
Fl.
Picc.
Ob.
Cl.
Bsn.
1-2
Hn.
3-4
a 2
Tpt.
Cnt.
1-2
Tbn.
3
B. Tbn.
Timp.
181
1
Vn.
2
Va.
Vc.
D.B.

Ensemble

38

43

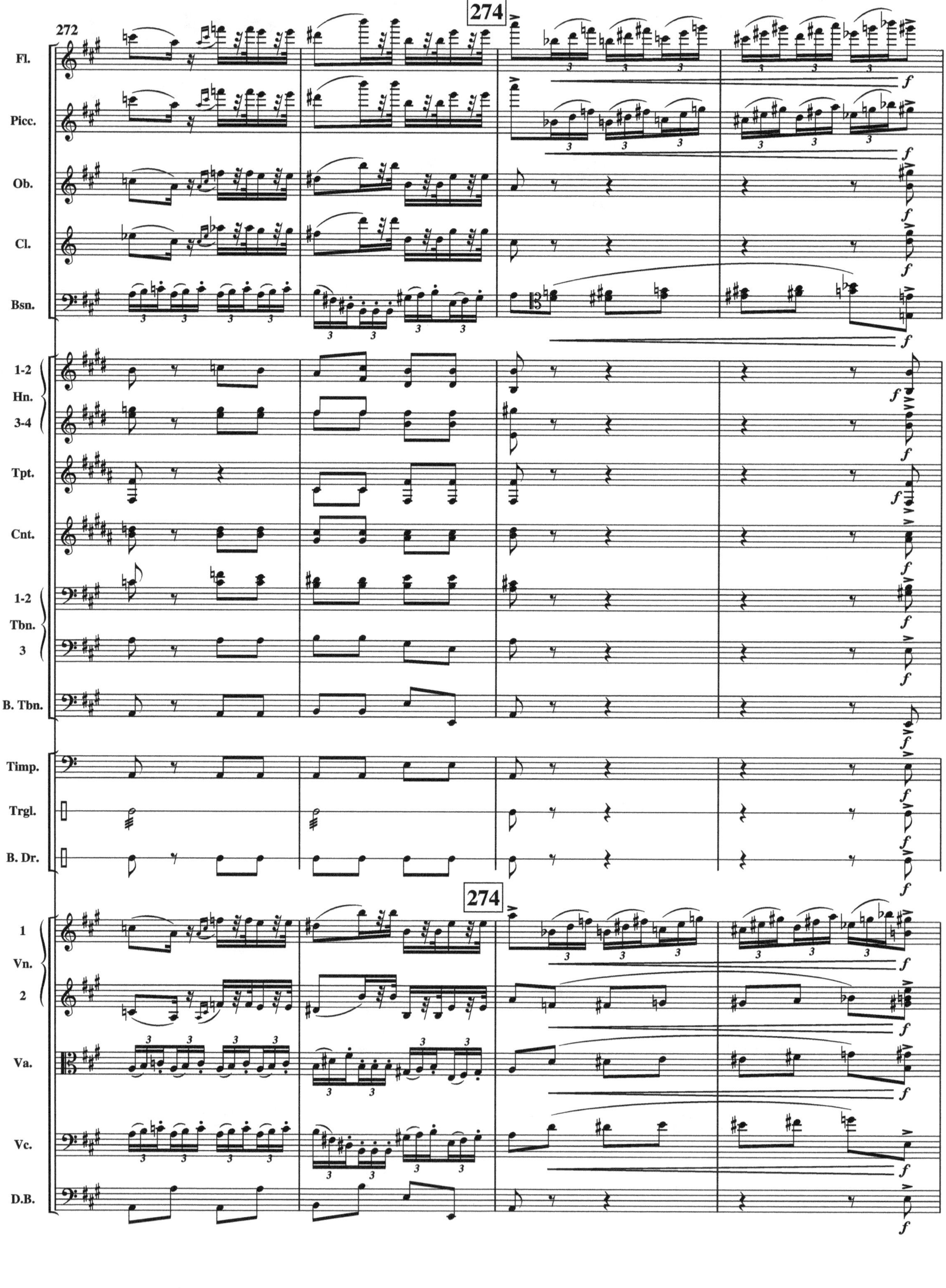
272
274
Fl.
Picc.
Ob.
Cl.
Bsn.
1-2
Hn.
3-4
Tpt.
Cnt.
1-2
Tbn.
3
B. Tbn.
Timp.
Trgl.
B. Dr.
274
1
Vn.
2
Va.
Vc.
D.B.
f

2. Seviliana

50

54

Echo de la vivandière

67

68

Echo du soldat

76

86

3. La Bohèmienne

100

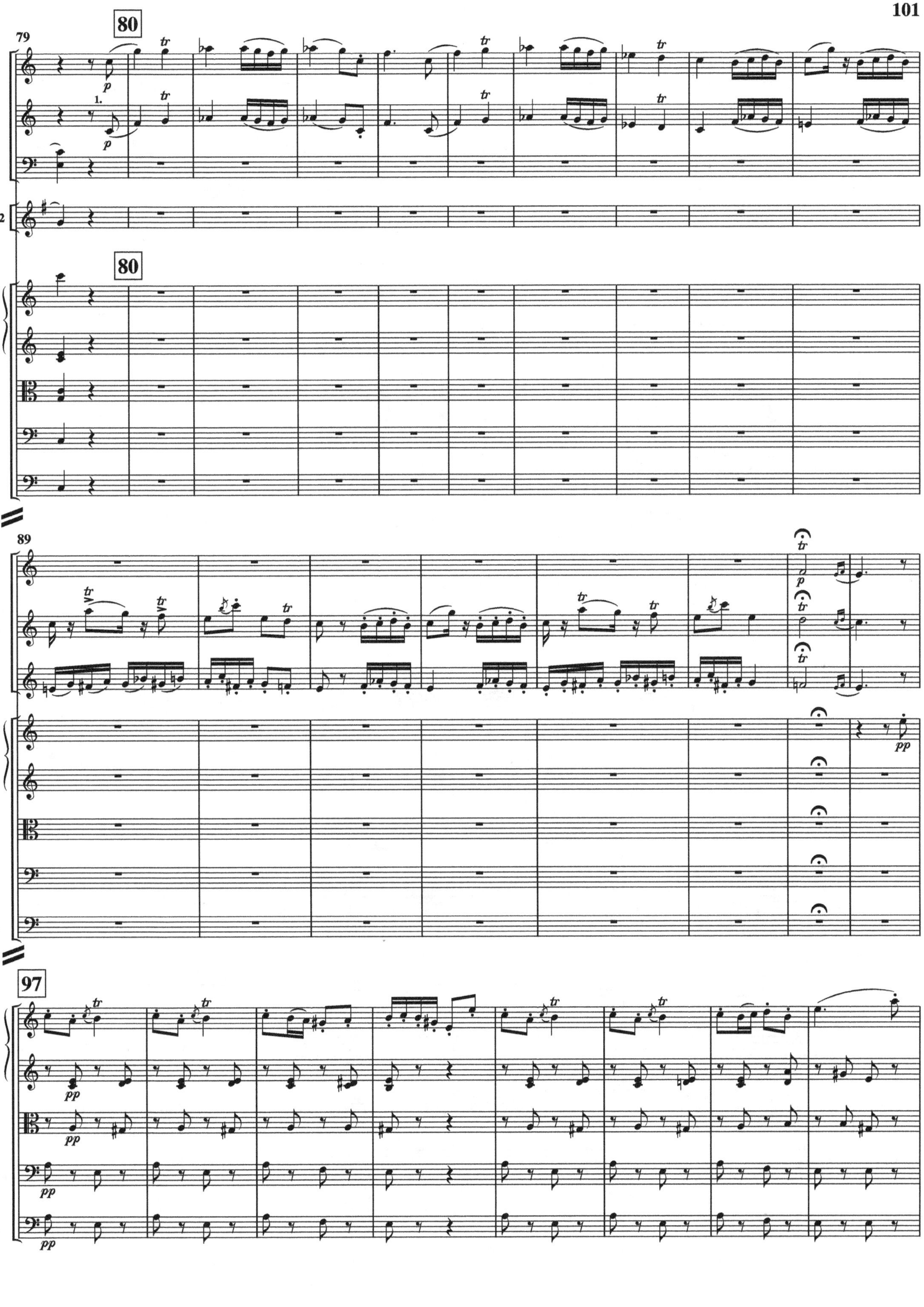
79
80
Picc.
Ob.
Bsn.
Hn. 1-2
1
Vn.
2
Va.
Vc.
D.B.
89
Fl.
97
tr
p
pp

104

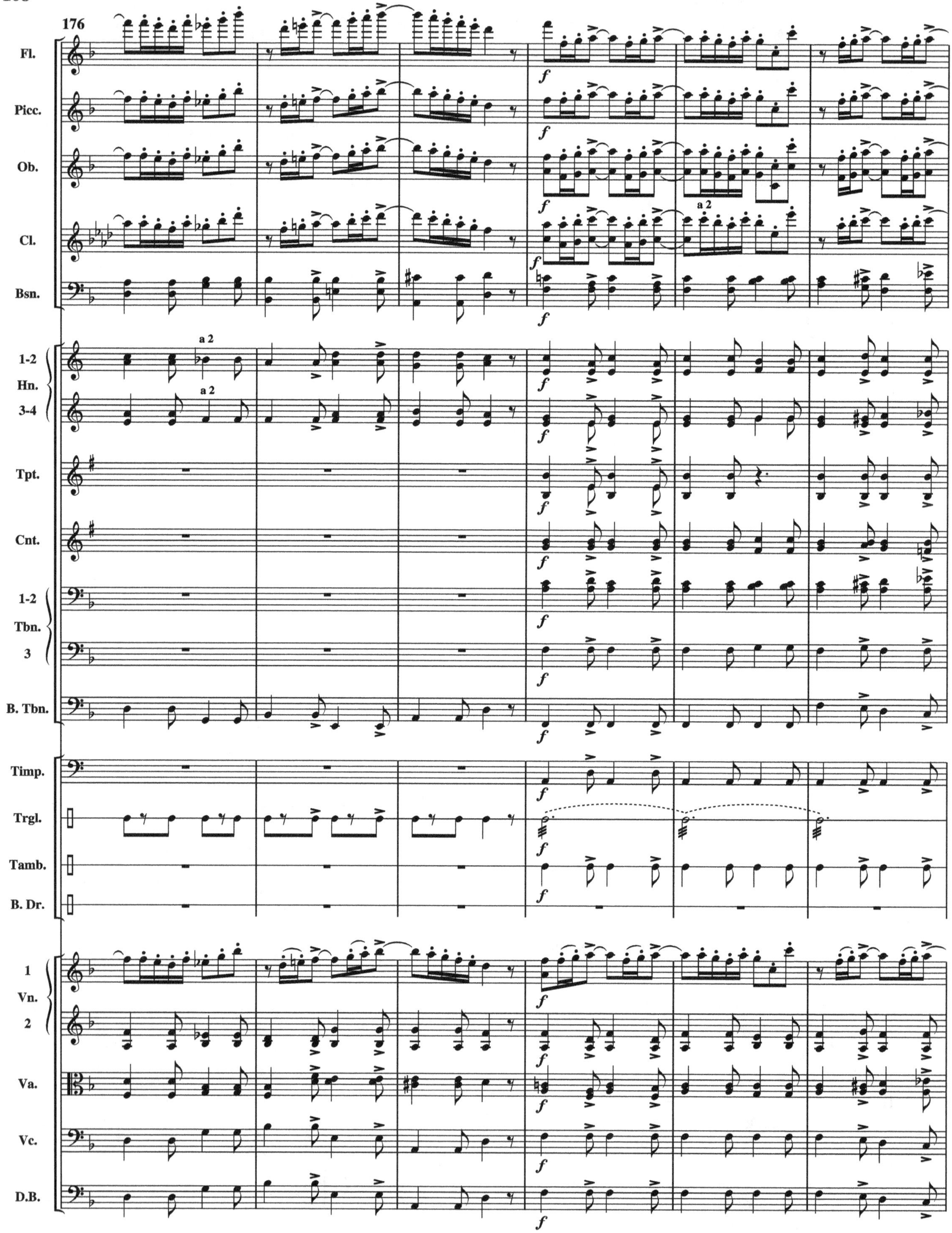
176
Fl.
Picc.
Ob.
Cl.
a 2
Bsn.
1-2
Hn.
3-4
a 2
a 2
Tpt.
Cnt.
1-2
Tbn.
3
B. Tbn.
Timp.
Trgl.
Tamb.
B. Dr.
1
Vn.
2
Va.
Vc.
D.B.
f

110

Echo de la Bohèmienne

Solo de la Bohèmienne

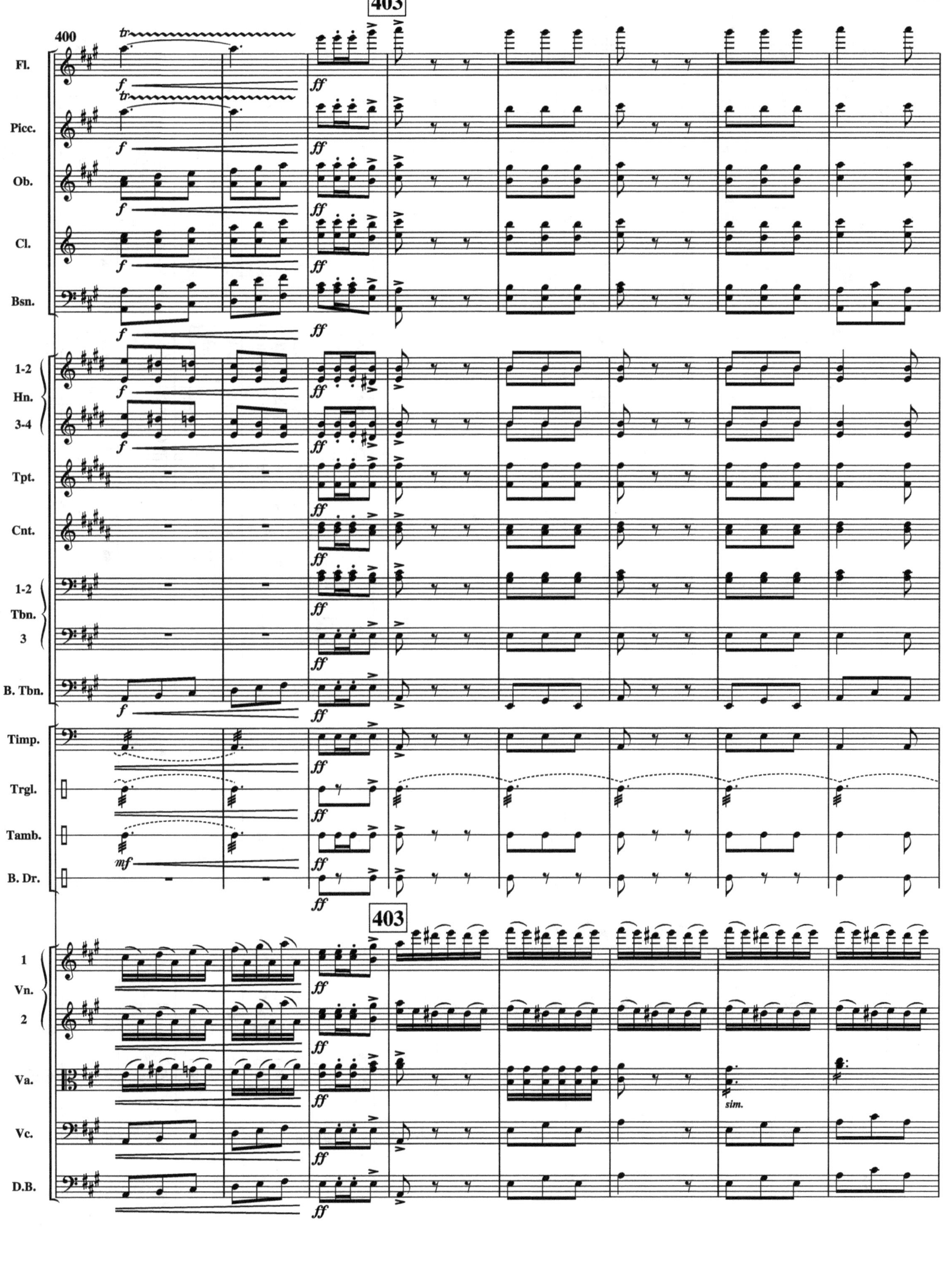
403
400
Fl.
Picc.
Ob.
Cl.
Bsn.
1-2
Hn.
3-4
Tpt.
Cnt.
1-2
Tbn.
3
B. Tbn.
Timp.
Trgl.
Tamb.
B. Dr.
403
1
Vn.
2
Va.
Vc.
D.B.
tr
f
ff
mf
sim.

4. Galop

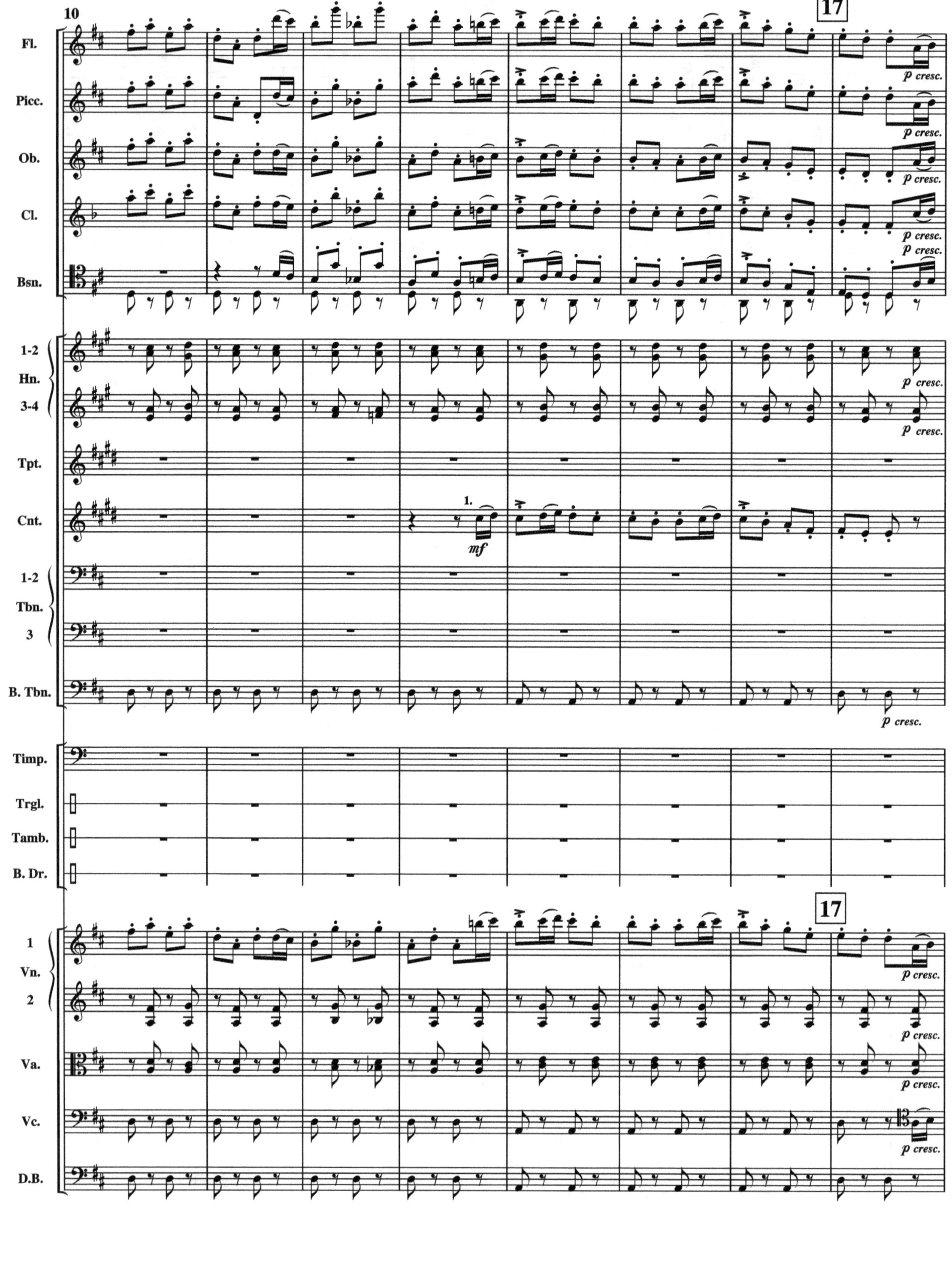
10
17
Fl.
Picc.
Ob.
Cl.
Bsn.
1-2
Hn.
3-4
Tpt.
Cnt.
1.
mf
1-2
Tbn.
3
B. Tbn.
Timp.
Trgl.
Tamb.
B. Dr.
17
1
Vn.
2
Va.
Vc.
D.B.
p cresc.

135

136

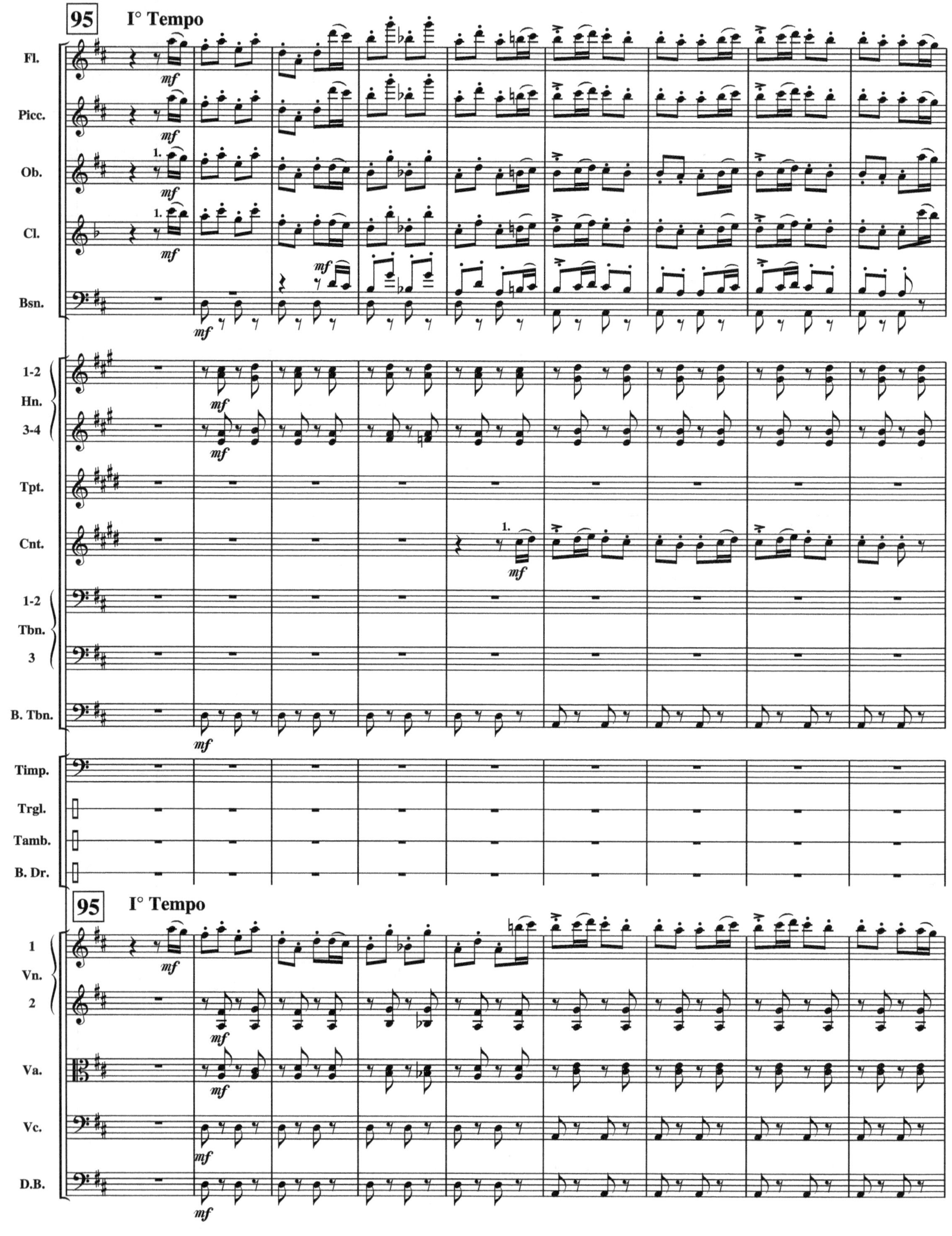
95
I° Tempo
Fl.
Picc.
Ob.
Cl.
Bsn.
1-2
Hn.
3-4
Tpt.
Cnt.
1-2
Tbn.
3
B. Tbn.
Timp.
Trgl.
Tamb.
B. Dr.
95
I° Tempo
1
Vn.
2
Va.
Vc.
D.B.

148

www.ingramcontent.com/pod-product-compliance
Lightning Source LLC
Chambersburg PA
CBHW080452170426
43196CB00016B/2767